Transformational Leadership

Alejandro Rivera

/ Alejandro Rivera /

Introduction to Transformational Leadership

In the dynamic landscape of business and society, a leadership approach emerges that goes beyond mere management and direction. We refer to Transformational Leadership, a paradigm that not only seeks to achieve goals and objectives, but aspires to inspire, motivate and elevate those they lead to new heights of achievement and development.

In this book, we embark on a journey of discovery into the complexities and wonders of Transformational Leadership. We will explore not only its theoretical foundations, but also its practical application in a variety of contexts. From classrooms to boardrooms, from small teams to entire organizations, Transformational Leadership is presented as a powerful force capable of not only managing change, but catalyzing significant transformations.

Throughout these pages, we will examine the distinctive characteristics of transformational leaders, their ability to inspire and motivate, as well as their ability to cultivate an environment conducive to innovation and growth. We will see how transformational leadership is not just a set of skills, but a philosophy that challenges convention and constantly seeks ways to improve and evolve.

Let's embark together on this fascinating leadership journey, where we will discover that true transformation begins with the leader and spreads, like shock waves, to all corners of the organization and beyond. Transformational Leadership is not just a theory; is a call to action for all those who wish to not only lead, but inspire, not only manage, but transform. Welcome to a new horizon of leadership!

The Fundamentals of Effective Leadership

Effective leadership is built on solid pillars that transcend fads and changing circumstances. Achieving mastery in leading teams and inspiring individuals requires a deep understanding of the essential fundamentals of leadership. This chapter dives into those foundations, outlining the universal principles that underpin all effective leadership.

1. Clear and Shared Vision

An effective leader articulates a compelling vision and communicates it in a way that inspires others. This vision not only guides actions, but also creates a sense of shared purpose and direction.

2. Skilled Communication

Effective communication is the glue that holds a team together. From active listening to clearly expressing ideas, a master leader masters the art of communication in all its forms.

3. Resilient Decision Making

Leadership involves making decisions, often at crucial moments. An effective leader does not fear making decisions, but embraces responsibility and learns from each choice, whether they will be a success or a challenge.

4. Development of Interpersonal Skills

The ability to understand and connect with people is essential. Effective leaders cultivate strong relationships and foster an environment of trust and collaboration.

5. Adaptability and Resilience

In an ever-changing world, effective leaders are able to adapt to new circumstances and overcome obstacles with resilience. The ability to lead through adversity defines a true leader.

6. Empathy and Recognition

Recognizing the contributions of others and demonstrating empathy toward individual needs and challenges strengthens team bonds and promotes a sense of belonging.

7. Talent Development

Nurturing and developing talent within the team is a constant commitment. An effective leader not only guides, but also invests in the professional growth and development of team members.

This chapter serves as a solid foundation for those seeking to understand and apply the essential foundations of effective leadership. As we continue on this journey, we are reminded that lasting leadership is built on these timeless principles.

/ Alejandro Rivera /

Key Characteristics of the Transformational Leader

Transformational leadership is a leadership style that focuses on inspiring and motivating team members to achieve goals beyond what is expected. Here are some key characteristics of the transformational leader:

Inspiring Vision

Transformational leaders have a clear and exciting vision of the future. They communicate this vision convincingly, inspiring others to follow them.

Charisma

Charisma is a distinctive quality of transformational leaders. They have the ability to attract and captivate people, generating a strong sense of identification and loyalty.

personal inspiration

These leaders not only talk about the vision, but also embody the desired values and behaviors. They serve as role models and motivate others to reach their full potential.

Intellectual Stimulus

They foster creativity and innovation by challenging conventional thinking and encouraging team members to question assumptions and seek new solutions.

Individualized consideration

They recognize and respond to the individual needs of team members. They care about the personal and professional development of each person, promoting an environment of support and trust.

Empowerment and Delegation

They foster a sense of autonomy and empowerment by delegating responsibilities. They allow team members to make decisions and take an active role in achieving goals.

Change management

Transformational leaders are skilled at managing change. They see challenges as opportunities and motivate others to embrace and adapt to positive changes.

Effective communication

They have exceptional communication skills. They know how to articulate vision and objectives clearly and persuasively, connecting emotionally with others.

Long-Term Results Orientation

Although they may address short-term goals, transformational leaders are oriented toward long-term goals. Their focus goes beyond simply meeting immediate goals.

Team Development

They focus on developing and strengthening the team. They build strong relationships and foster a collaborative environment where each member feels valued and contributes to collective success.

These key characteristics work together to create an environment where followers feel inspired, motivated, and empowered to achieve extraordinary goals.

Leadership Models in History

Throughout history, there have been various leadership models that have emerged in different cultural, political and social contexts. Some of these leadership models have left a significant mark on the way we understand and practice leadership. Here are some examples:

Charismatic Leadership - Mahatma Gandhi

Gandhi was a charismatic leader who inspired millions of people in India through his nonviolent actions. His charisma lay in his firmness of principle, his dedication to justice, and his ability to mobilize the masses peacefully.

Transformational Leadership - Martin Luther King Jr.

King was a key transformational leader in the civil rights movement in the United States. His ability to articulate an inspiring vision and mobilize people toward common goals makes him an example of transformational leadership.

Situational Leadership - Dwight D. Eisenhower

Eisenhower, a general and president of the United States, is often associated with situational leadership. He had the ability to adapt to different situations and adjust his leadership style according to the demands of the moment, whether on the battlefield or in politics.

Autocratic Leadership - Adolf Hitler

Hitler is an example of autocratic leadership, where power is concentrated in a single central figure and decisions are made in an authoritarian manner. This style of leadership had devastating consequences during World War II.

Democratic Leadership - Nelson Mandela

Mandela, the anti-apartheid leader and former president of South Africa, is often seen as an example of democratic leadership. He advocated reconciliation and unity at a crucial time in South African history.

Charismatic and Visionary Leadership - Steve Jobs

Jobs, co-founder of Apple, was known for his charismatic leadership and his ability to envision innovative products. His often challenging style and focus on excellence have left a significant mark on the world of technology.

Transactional Leadership - Jack Welch

Welch was the CEO of General Electric and is often associated with transactional leadership. This approach involves exchanging rewards and punishments based on performance, and Welch was known for his focus on results and efficiency.

These are just a few examples, and it is important to note that leadership effectiveness often depends on specific context and circumstances. Additionally, some leaders may incorporate elements of various leadership styles into their approach.

Inspiration and Motivation

Influencing the inspiration and motivation of others requires empathy, effective communication skills, and positive leadership. Here are some strategies you can employ to inspire and motivate others:

Clear Communication of Vision

Clear communication of vision is essential for effective leadership, as it involves conveying the strategic direction, objectives and mission of an organization in a way that inspires and motivates others. The vision should be clear, meaningful and exciting, articulating where the organization is headed and the positive impact it hopes to achieve. By relating the vision to the organization's core values, the emotional connection to the mission is strengthened.

It is crucial to communicate the vision consistently, repeating and reinforcing the message so that the vision takes root in people's minds and becomes a constant guide. The language used should be inspiring, using words and phrases that evoke positive emotions and convey the importance and urgency of the vision. Painting vivid mental images that represent the realization of the vision helps people visualize success and make the connection between their daily work and the end goal.

Participation and feedback are key to engaging team members in the vision. Adapting the message according to the audience ensures that the communication is relevant and understandable to different groups. Relating the vision to each individual's daily work highlights the importance of each contribution and reinforces the sense of purpose. Being prepared to address questions and concerns, as well as celebrating successes and successes along the way, helps maintain motivation and engagement.

Reviewing and updating the vision as necessary is essential as circumstances evolve. Clear communication of vision, when done effectively, becomes a powerful tool for aligning a team and motivating them toward achieving shared goals. An effective leader not only formulates an inspiring vision, but also communicates it in a way that resonates with the aspirations and values of his team.

Model Desired Behavior

Be a role model. Practice the attitudes and behaviors you expect to see in others. Consistency between your words and actions builds confidence and motivation.

Recognition and Appreciation

Recognition and appreciation in the work environment are essential components to foster a positive and motivating environment. Recognizing work well done involves more than simply pointing out achievements; It involves authentically expressing the value and contribution of team members. This recognition can take various forms, from public praise to awards, but its impact lies in the genuine gesture of appreciation for effort and dedication.

Timely recognition is especially crucial. When achieving a goal or overcoming challenges is recognized, positive behavior is reinforced and employees are motivated to maintain high levels of performance. This type of positive feedback also contributes to building an organizational culture where excellence is valued and celebrated, generating a cycle of continuous motivation.

In addition to highlighting individual achievements, it is important to recognize collaborative efforts. Doing so strengthens the sense of belonging to the team and fosters a culture of mutual support. This type of recognition also helps cement the idea that success is a collective effort and that each team member plays a valuable role in achieving shared goals.

Recognition and appreciation are not limited to big victories; Even small achievements or improvements deserve to be recognized. This creates an environment where employees consistently feel valued, which has a positive impact on morale, job satisfaction, and talent retention. Ultimately, effective recognition and appreciation contributes not only to short-term motivation, but also to the overall well-being and long-term engagement of team members.

Foster a Positive Environment

Fostering a positive atmosphere in the work environment is essential to cultivating the motivation and productivity of team members. This environment is built on the foundation of healthy working relationships, where open communication and mutual respect are essential. When leaders set a positive tone, it creates a ripple effect that influences the attitude and behavior of the entire team.

Promoting a positive environment involves recognizing and celebrating achievements, even small advances, thereby highlighting progress and fostering a sense of accomplishment. At the same time, it is important to approach challenges with a constructive mindset, viewing difficulties as opportunities to learn and grow rather than insurmountable obstacles. This contributes to resilience and the willingness to face new challenges.

Inclusion and diversity also play a crucial role in a positive work environment. When you value diversity of perspectives, skills and experiences, you create a space where all employees feel respected and appreciated. This sense of belonging strengthens team cohesion and promotes an environment where each individual feels free to contribute their unique ideas and skills.

Transparency in communication and decision making is another key element in fostering positivity. When employees feel that they are informed and are part of the decision-making process, an environment of trust is built. Additionally, constructive feedback becomes a valuable tool for personal and professional growth, as it is given in a way that inspires improvement rather than demotivation.

Ultimately, fostering a positive environment involves cultivating an organizational culture where work is perceived as meaningful, where collaboration is encouraged, and where gratitude and recognition are everyday practices. This type of environment not only contributes to the general well-being of employees, but also enhances the team's creativity, innovation, and effectiveness in achieving common goals.

Delegation and Empowerment

Delegate responsibilities and empower others. Allowing them to take on important roles and make decisions contributes to a sense of responsibility and motivation.

Set Clear Expectations

Setting clear expectations is a critical component of effective leadership, as it provides team members with clear guidance about what is expected of them. Clarity around objectives, responsibilities, and performance standards is essential to align everyone toward common goals. When leaders accurately and transparently communicate what is expected, it makes it easier for employees to understand their role and how their contribution contributes to overall success.

In addition to clarity in expectations, it is crucial to involve team members in the goal and objective setting process. When employees actively participate in defining their own goals and understand how they link to the overall vision of the organization, a deeper sense of purpose and motivation is created.

Setting expectations also involves providing constant feedback on performance. Leaders must be clear in communicating what is working well and where improvements can be made. This constructive feedback not only helps to correct course when necessary, but also reinforces positive behaviors and contributes to the continued development of employees.

In an environment where expectations are clear, employees feel more empowered to make informed decisions and take responsibility. Additionally, transparency about expectations creates an environment of trust and openness, where team members feel comfortable sharing their ideas and concerns without fear of misunderstanding.

Finally, setting clear expectations is not static. As circumstances and organizational goals evolve, expectations need to be proactively adjusted and communicated. Flexibility in this process ensures that the team is always aligned with strategic objectives and that team members are equipped to succeed in their work. In summary, clarity in expectations is a fundamental pillar for a well-organized and motivated team.

Offers Development Opportunities

Offering development opportunities is a key strategy for keeping team members motivated and engaged. This involves providing pathways for employees to grow professionally and personally, fostering an environment in which continuous improvement is valued and encouraged. Providing development opportunities not only benefits individual employees, but also contributes to the long-term success of the organization.

Professional development can take many forms, from training programs and workshops to challenging assignments and special projects. By offering these opportunities, leaders demonstrate a commitment to the growth and evolution of their team. Additionally, access to educational resources and training strengthens employees' skills and competency, allowing them to contribute more meaningfully to the achievement of organizational goals.

Likewise, providing opportunities for personal development is essential. This may include mentoring programs, coaching, or activities that encourage work-life balance. When employees feel that the organization cares about their overall well-being, they are more inclined to dedicate themselves fully to their job responsibilities.

Personalization in development opportunities is also crucial. Recognizing and supporting each team member's individual growth goals allows for a more tailored approach to their specific needs and aspirations. This not only maximizes the impact of development, but also strengthens employee commitment and loyalty to the organization.

An important aspect of development is the recognition of achievements made during the process. Celebrating developmental milestones reinforces the importance of continuous learning and motivates others to seek similar opportunities. Ultimately, offering development opportunities not only enhances skills and competencies, but also nurtures a culture of learning and growth within the team, contributing to long-term success at both an individual and organizational level.

Promotes Collaboration

Promoting collaboration in the work environment is essential to fostering a strong and efficient team. Collaboration goes beyond simply working together; involves creating an environment where team members feel comfortable sharing ideas, knowledge, and resources to achieve common goals. When leaders actively promote collaboration, they are building the foundation of a team that can address challenges together and leverage diversity of skills and perspectives.

Collaboration fosters creativity and innovation by promoting a free exchange of ideas. When employees feel that their opinions are valued and that they have a space to contribute, an environment conducive to the generation of novel solutions and continuous process improvement is created.

Additionally, collaboration contributes to building strong relationships between team members. When employees work together on projects and share responsibilities, mutual trust is strengthened. This not only improves team dynamics, but also facilitates open communication and effective conflict resolution.

Promoting collaboration may also involve implementing tools and technologies that facilitate communication and information sharing. Collaborative platforms and regular meetings to discuss ideas and projects are effective ways to keep everyone on the team informed and engaged.

Cross-functional collaboration between departments and hierarchical levels is also key to maximizing the team's potential. By breaking down organizational barriers and fostering collaboration between different areas, a more comprehensive and efficient approach is promoted to address challenges and achieve strategic goals.

In short, promoting collaboration not only improves operational effectiveness, but also contributes to a nurturing work environment. When leaders foster a collaborative spirit, they are cultivating a team that can adapt to rapid change, navigate complex challenges, and thrive in an increasingly interconnected world of work.

Active listening

Listen to your colleagues. Understanding their concerns, ideas, and aspirations can help you adapt your leadership approach to meet their needs and motivations.

Celebrate Successes

Celebrate achievements, even small ones. Recognizing and celebrating successes creates a positive environment and reinforces the idea that worthwhile effort leads to positive results.

Provide Constructive Feedback

Provides constructive and development-oriented feedback. Helps people understand how they can improve and grow in their roles.

Remember that each person is unique, so it's important to tailor your approach to the individual needs of your team members. Authenticity and empathy are key to positively influencing the inspiration and motivation of others.

/ Alejandro Rivera /

Development of Vision and Transformational Strategy

The development of a transformational vision and strategy involves a deep process of reflection and planning that will guide the future direction of the organization. It begins by identifying the entity's core values and essential mission, outlining an inspiring vision that reflects the desired destination. This vision must be clear, compelling and capable of inspiring all team members, providing a collective sense of purpose.

Together with the vision, a transformational strategy is developed that charts the path to achieve these ambitious objectives. This strategy involves a deep analysis of the external and internal environment, identifying opportunities and challenges, as well as the distinctive capabilities of the organization. Additionally, market trends, emerging technologies and changing stakeholder needs are considered to ensure long-term relevance.

The active participation of team members is essential in this process. Collaboration is encouraged to gather diverse perspectives and harness collective intelligence. Leaders not only communicate vision and strategy, but also integrate it into the organizational culture, ensuring that every decision and action is aligned with transformational objectives.

The execution of the transformational strategy involves a proactive approach to change management, as it seeks to challenge the status quo and embrace new ways of thinking and working. Training and skills development are integrated to align employees with the vision and ensure they are equipped to contribute to positive change. Constant measurement of progress and agile adaptation are key elements to adjusting strategy as needed in a dynamic environment.

Ultimately, the development of transformational vision and strategy is not just a strategic exercise, but an invitation to the organization to embark on a journey of continuous evolution, where adaptability and innovation are fundamental to achieving ambitious and sustainable goals.

Developing a transformational vision and strategy requires careful reflection on the fundamental purpose of the organization and the direction it seeks to follow. In this process, leaders not only identify tangible goals and objectives, but also seek to understand the essence of what the organization aspires to achieve and how it will positively impact its environment.

A transformational vision must go beyond simply describing the future; must inspire and motivate all team members. It seeks to create a vivid and exciting image of future success, connecting strategic goals with the organization's core values. The vision acts as a beacon that guides decisions and actions, providing a moral compass for the company.

The transformational strategy, on the other hand, involves the formulation of concrete plans to achieve the vision. This includes identifying key initiatives, allocating resources, and defining success indicators. The strategy must be agile and adaptive, capable of responding to changes in the business environment and new opportunities that arise.

Effective communication plays a crucial role in this process. Leaders must articulate the vision and strategy clearly and persuasively, ensuring that all team members understand their role in realizing these ambitious goals. Transparency and openness to dialogue are essential to foster understanding and commitment.

The successful implementation of a transformational strategy involves strengthening the organizational culture. Desired values and behaviors are reinforced through leadership practices, reward systems, and development programs. The ability to learn and adapt becomes a core competency for all team members.

In summary, developing transformational vision and strategy is not only a strategic exercise, but a holistic process that encompasses inspiration, detailed planning and efficient execution. It requires ongoing commitment from all levels of the organization to achieve meaningful and lasting change.

Transformational Communication: How to Inspire through Words

Transformational communication, focused on inspiring through words, involves a conscious and authentic approach to motivating and mobilizing others. First, it is essential to cultivate empathy, understanding the audience's perspectives and emotions. This knowledge allows you to adapt the message in a way that resonates with your values and aspirations, creating an emotional connection.

The use of inspiring language is essential. Words must go beyond the mere transmission of information; They should evoke emotions and trigger a sense of shared purpose. Clarity in the articulation of vision and goals, combined with powerful metaphors and narratives, helps paint a vivid picture of the desired future, motivating action.

Authenticity is the cornerstone of transformational communication. Leaders must speak from the heart, sharing their own experiences and values. This level of authenticity not only builds trust, but also inspires others to be more open and engaged. Transparency about the challenges and path to success reinforces the credibility of the message.

Open, two-way dialogue is essential. Transformational communication is not a monologue; It is a continuous exchange. Fostering an environment where opinions are valued and active participation is encouraged contributes to constructive dialogue, generating a sense of belonging and collectivity.

Finally, consistency in message over time is key. The repetition of fundamental themes reinforces the importance of vision and strategy, anchoring the shared purpose in the minds of the audience. Consistency between words and actions supports credibility and strengthens the transformational impact of communication. Together, these elements create communication that not only informs, but also inspires, guiding individuals and teams toward achieving meaningful, shared goals.

Transformational communication, intended to inspire through words, requires a strategic approach that goes beyond the mere transmission of information. First of all, it is essential to establish an emotional connection with the audience. This is achieved by acknowledging and validating your emotions, concerns and aspirations. Showing empathy and understanding establishes common ground to build a powerful and resonant message.

Effective transformational communication also involves presenting a clear and ambitious vision. Leaders must articulate not only the "what," that is, concrete goals, but also the "why," highlighting the relevance and deeper purpose behind these goals. This compelling vision acts like a magnet, attracting the audience's attention and adherence.

Using metaphors and analogies can be a powerful tool to illustrate complex concepts and make insight more accessible. Evocative images and inspiring stories help paint a vivid picture of the desired future, facilitating understanding and generating lasting emotional impact.

In transformational communication, authenticity is an invaluable asset. Leaders must be genuine and transparent in their expression, sharing personal experiences and demonstrating an authentic connection to the vision they are presenting. This authenticity creates fertile ground for trust and credibility.

Furthermore, encouraging active participation and continuous dialogue is essential. Communication should not be limited to a single address; It is a dynamic exchange. By inviting your audience to contribute ideas and perspectives, you build a sense of collectivity and belonging, strengthening engagement and motivation.

In short, transformational communication goes beyond informing; seeks to inspire, mobilize and connect people with a shared purpose. With a strategic approach that incorporates emotional, narrative and participatory elements, this form of communication has the power to catalyze significant and lasting changes in individuals and teams.

/ Alejandro Rivera /

The Importance of Emotional Intelligence in Leadership

The importance of emotional intelligence in leadership lies in its ability to strengthen interpersonal relationships and enhance team performance. Leaders with high emotional intelligence possess a deep understanding of their own emotions, allowing them to manage stress and make informed decisions in challenging situations. Additionally, this skill extends to perceiving and understanding the emotions of others, fostering empathy and the ability to adapt to the individual needs of team members.

The ability to regulate and express emotions effectively is key to leadership. Emotionally intelligent leaders can manage conflict constructively, motivate their teams, and create a positive work environment. Empathy, a central component of emotional intelligence, allows leaders to understand the concerns and perspectives of their collaborators, thus building stronger relationships and an organizational culture based on trust and collaboration.

Additionally, emotional intelligence influences decision making, as leaders can more accurately assess the emotional impact of their choices on the team. This emotional awareness translates into greater effectiveness in inspiring and motivating, contributing to overall engagement and productivity. In summary, emotional intelligence in leadership not only improves team dynamics, but also enhances the ability to lead in changing and challenging environments.

Emotional intelligence in leadership plays a fundamental role in positively influencing the organizational climate and leadership effectiveness. Emotionally intelligent leaders are able to manage their own emotions in a way that not only maintains personal balance, but also sets a positive emotional tone in the work environment. This self-regulation skill contributes to a healthier and more collaborative work environment.

Likewise, emotional intelligence facilitates the building of solid relationships between leaders and their teams. Empathy, one of the key dimensions of emotional intelligence, allows leaders to understand the experiences and perspectives of their collaborators, strengthening interpersonal connection. This connection, in turn, fosters trust and loyalty, essential elements for effective long-term leadership.

The ability to motivate and inspire is another area where emotional intelligence stands out. Emotionally intelligent leaders are skilled at recognizing and rewarding achievements, providing emotional stimulation that drives team members' intrinsic motivation. This ability to lead with emotion and purpose contributes to a sense of meaning at work, improving job satisfaction and talent retention.

In times of change and adversity, emotional intelligence becomes even more critical. Emotionally intelligent leaders are able to manage the emotional impact of challenging situations, maintaining emotional stability and guiding their teams toward constructive solutions. Emotional resilience becomes an invaluable asset to overcome obstacles and lead successfully in difficult conditions.

In short, emotional intelligence not only improves the leader's personal skills, but also has a direct impact on team dynamics and organizational culture. By integrating emotional awareness into leadership, you establish a solid foundation for personal and professional growth, as well as sustainable organizational success.

/ Alejandro Rivera /

Empathy as a Transformation Tool

Empathy functions as a powerful transformation tool by enabling a deep understanding of the experiences and perspectives of others. In the context of leadership and organizational change, empathy becomes a catalyst for transformation by facilitating genuine connection between leaders and team members. When leaders practice empathy, they show genuine concern for employees' emotions, challenges, and aspirations, thereby building stronger, trust-based relationships.

Empathy acts as a bridge that connects people and promotes a sense of belonging. In situations of change, where uncertainties and resistance may arise, empathy serves as a mechanism to validate individual concerns and dissolve possible barriers. Empathetic leaders not only understand their teams' emotional reactions to change, but also adapt their approaches and messages to address those emotions, paving the way for more effective transformation.

Additionally, empathy facilitates the creation of an inclusive environment, where each team member feels valued and understood. This encourages diversity of thought and promotes innovation, key elements for any successful transformation process. Empathetic leaders not only listen, but also act on the needs and concerns of their team, showing a real commitment to their well-being and development.

Ultimately, empathy as a tool for transformation goes beyond mere understanding; drives positive action and strengthens team cohesion. By cultivating an organizational culture based on empathy, leaders can lead change processes more effectively, building resilient and adaptive teams that embrace transformation with a shared sense of purpose and mutual support.

Empathy operates as a transformation tool by facilitating a deep emotional connection between leaders and teams, generating an environment conducive to positive change. In the context of organizational transformation, empathy is manifested by understanding employees' anxieties and resistance to change. Empathic leaders recognize and validate these concerns, which contributes to the creation of a safe space for the expression of emotions, thus paving the way for a smoother and more effective transition.

Empathy also plays a critical role in stimulating creativity and collaboration during transformation processes. By understanding the unique perspectives and skills of team members, leaders can assign roles and responsibilities more strategically, leveraging individual strengths for the collective benefit. This deep understanding fosters an environment where innovative ideas flourish and a culture of continuous learning is promoted.

Likewise, empathy as a transformation tool is reflected in the ability of leaders to adapt their communication strategies. By understanding how messages may be perceived emotionally by different audiences, leaders can adjust their approach to address specific employee concerns, thereby building a sense of collectivity around transformation goals.

Empathy is not only limited to understanding, but also drives action. Empathic leaders are best positioned to implement support measures and resources that address the emotional and professional needs of their teams during periods of change. This proactive action reinforces trust and demonstrates a genuine commitment to employee well-being and development.

In short, empathy not only serves as a means to understanding, but as a driver for transformative action. By incorporating empathy into leadership during change processes, an environment is created that favors adaptability, innovation and collaboration, essential elements for a successful and sustainable organizational transformation.

/ Alejandro Rivera /

Crisis and Transformational Leadership

Applying transformational leadership in times of crisis involves taking a proactive and visionary approach to guiding the organization through significant challenges. First, transformational leaders must communicate a clear, inspiring vision that transcends immediate adversity, providing team members with a sense of purpose and direction. This visionary approach acts as a beacon that guides decisions and actions during the crisis.

Empathy becomes an essential tool in transformational leadership during difficult times. Leaders must demonstrate understanding and sensitivity to employees' individual concerns and challenges, creating an emotionally supportive environment. By displaying authenticity and concern for the well-being of their team, transformational leaders build strong relationships that strengthen group cohesion and resilience.

Stimulating innovation and creativity is another key aspect of transformational leadership in crisis. Fostering an environment where new ideas are valued and creative solutions are sought contribute to adaptability and the emergence of opportunities in the midst of adversity. Transformational leaders motivate their teams to think beyond current limitations, seeking innovative ways to overcome challenges and transform crisis into an opportunity for growth and learning.

Finally, authenticity and transparency in communication are essential. Transformational leaders recognize the realities of the crisis, but also highlight the potential of overcoming it together. Sharing relevant information and being honest about challenges as well as action plans fosters trust and collaboration.

In crisis situations, transformational leadership excels by focusing on inspiring and mobilizing teams toward adaptation and positive change. Transformational leaders become motivational agents, encouraging team members to overcome adversity by creating a collective sense of urgency and purpose. This involves setting challenging but achievable goals, focusing on innovation and creative problem solving to address the specific challenges that the crisis poses.

Flexibility and the ability to lead through ambiguity are crucial aspects of transformational leadership in critical moments. Leaders must be able to adjust strategies and priorities as circumstances evolve, while providing constant direction and a long-term vision. This adaptability translates into greater organizational resilience and the ability to take advantage of emerging opportunities even in the midst of turbulence.

Building strong relationships is intensified in transformational leadership during crisis. Leaders must connect on a personal level with team members, demonstrating support and understanding not only of work demands, but also personal and emotional concerns. This connection strengthens team cohesion and fosters an environment of trust and solidarity.

Transformational leadership in crisis also involves making bold and ethical decisions. Leaders must be able to quickly evaluate available options, make informed decisions, and take responsibility for their choices. Transparency about the decision-making process and a willingness to learn from the results, whether successes or failures, contribute to leadership credibility.

In conclusion, transformational crisis leadership is characterized by inspiration, adaptability, relationship building, and bold decision making. These aspects work together to not only guide the organization through the crisis, but also position it for innovation and long-term sustainable growth.

/ Alejandro Rivera /

Transformational Leadership in Multicultural Teams

Applying transformational leadership in multicultural teams requires an adaptive approach and a deep understanding of the cultural differences present. First, transformational leaders must foster inclusion and diversity, recognizing and valuing the different perspectives and skills brought by each team member. This involves cultivating an environment where cultural differences are celebrated and mutual respect is promoted.

Effective communication becomes even more crucial in multicultural teams. Transformational leaders must be aware of language barriers and differences in communication styles, adapting their approach to ensure the message is understandable and resonates with all team members. Transparency and openness in communication contribute to building an environment of trust, essential for transformational leadership.

Encouraging creativity and innovation is essential in multicultural teams, as diversity of perspectives can lead to richer and more creative solutions. Transformational leaders must foster an environment that values the unique contribution of each member, encouraging active participation and the free expression of ideas. The ability to inspire and motivate through shared vision becomes even more vital in this context, as a common purpose can overcome cultural differences and unify the team towards shared goals.

Furthermore, transformational leadership in multicultural teams involves the development of cultural intelligence. Leaders must educate themselves on the various cultures present on the team, understand the underlying cultural dynamics, and adjust their leadership strategies as necessary. Cultural sensitivity and adaptability are essential to building effective relationships and leading a diverse team toward collective achievement of goals.

Transformational leadership in multicultural teams is also highlighted by building an inclusive environment that fosters collaboration and intercultural understanding. Transformational leaders must actively promote the integration of diverse cultures, establishing norms and practices that value equality and equity. By creating an environment where each member feels respected and recognized, team cohesion is strengthened and the possibility of cultural conflicts is reduced.

Flexibility and adaptability are essential in transformational leadership in multicultural contexts. Leaders must be willing to adjust their leadership methods based on the cultural needs and expectations of team members. This involves understanding differences in work styles, communication preferences, and attitudes toward authority. The ability to adapt to these cultural variations contributes to leadership effectiveness and building strong relationships.

The development of conflict management skills becomes crucial in multicultural teams under transformational leadership. Cultural differences can lead to misunderstandings or tensions, and leaders must be able to address these challenges constructively. Promoting open dialogue and facilitating culturally sensitive conflict resolution helps maintain team harmony.

Finally, celebrating diversity becomes a fundamental practice of transformational leadership in multicultural teams. Recognizing and highlighting the individual contributions of each member, as well as celebrating significant cultural events, promotes a feeling of belonging and enriches the work experience. Transformational leaders who foster an environment where diversity is appreciated and are considered contributors not only to the success of the team, but also to the individual and collective growth of its members.

/ Alejandro Rivera /

Ethics and Responsibility in Leadership

Ethics and responsibility are fundamental in leadership, acting as pillars that support the integrity and credibility of a leader. From an ethical perspective, leaders must make decisions based on solid moral principles and values, ensuring that their actions are aligned with high ethical standards. This involves not only complying with rules and regulations, but also going beyond, considering the impact of your decisions on all acceptable parties and seeking long-term well-being.

Responsibility in leadership involves assuming the consequences of the decisions made and the actions undertaken. Responsible leaders recognize that they have a crucial role in the success or failure of their teams or organizations and therefore must be held accountable for their choices. This includes a willingness to admit mistakes, learn from them, and take corrective action when necessary. In addition, it involves responsibility towards employees, customers and society in general, ensuring that business operations and practices are ethical, sustainable and socially responsible.

Together, ethics and responsibility in leadership form the basis of effective and sustainable leadership. Ethical and responsible leaders not only inspire trust and loyalty, but also contribute to the development of a positive work environment and the building of a strong and ethical business reputation. By prioritizing ethical decision-making and taking responsibility for their actions, leaders set a high standard that influences organizational culture and public perception of the company.

Ethics and responsibility in leadership also manifest in leaders' ability to act with integrity in all interactions. Integrity involves consistency between words and actions, as well as honesty and transparency in all operations. Ethical leaders set an example by adhering to moral principles, even in challenging situations, and by building relationships based on mutual trust with their teams and other stakeholders.

Likewise, corporate social responsibility (CSR) has become increasingly crucial in contemporary leadership. Ethical leaders recognize the significant influence they have on society and the environment, and take responsibility for contributing to general well-being. This involves considering the social and environmental impact of business operations, adopting sustainable practices and actively participating in community initiatives. CSR not only strengthens the company's image, but also reflects leadership committed to building a more just and sustainable world.

Ethics and responsibility also extend to the development and well-being of employees. Ethical leaders care about the professional and personal growth of their teams, offering development opportunities, a healthy work environment, and fair compensation. Equity in human resources practices and the promotion of diversity and inclusion are essential aspects of ethical responsibility in leadership.

In summary, ethics and responsibility in leadership encompass personal integrity, corporate social responsibility, and commitment to the well-being of employees. These aspects not only define a leader's identity and reputation, but also contribute to the creation of ethical and socially responsible organizations that thrive in the long term.

/ Alejandro Rivera /

The Leader as Mentor: Creating the Next Generation of Transformational Leaders

Creating new leaders involves a comprehensive focus on developing skills and promoting a leadership mindset from within the organization. First, it is essential to identify and cultivate the leadership potential among employees. This is achieved through assessment programs, mentoring and the assignment of challenging responsibilities that allow employees to demonstrate and develop their leadership skills.

Experiential learning plays a crucial role in training new leaders. Exposure to internship leadership situations, such as special projects or temporary leadership roles, provides opportunities to apply theories and skills in a real-world setting. Structured training programs that address specific skills, from decision making to change management, are also essential to building a strong foundation for emerging leadership.

Mentoring and coaching by established leaders offer a valuable path to developing new leaders. Mentors can provide personalized guidance, share experiences, and provide constructive feedback, accelerating the growth of those who are emerging as leaders. Additionally, fostering an environment that promotes collaboration and knowledge sharing between experienced and emerging leaders contributes to the effective transfer of skills and knowledge.

Creating new leaders also involves promoting a culture that values and rewards leadership. Recognize and celebrate the achievements of emerging leaders, as well as provide clear opportunities for advancement, encouraging others to take on leadership roles. Creating an environment that encourages initiative, creativity and risk-taking will support the continued development of new leaders and contribute to the sustainable growth of the organization.

Creating new leaders involves a strategic approach that goes beyond the development of technical skills, focusing on aspects such as emotional intelligence, empathy and effective people management. Promoting self-awareness and self-reflection is essential for future leaders to understand their strengths and areas of development. This can be achieved through assessments, 360-degree feedback and personalized development programs.

Exposure to different contexts and roles within the organization is a key component to developing versatile leaders with a holistic understanding. Job rotations, international assignments, and interdepartmental projects provide opportunities to gain a broad perspective and to develop leadership skills that transcend specific functions. This diversity of experiences prepares future leaders to face complex challenges and make informed decisions.

The promotion of innovation and creativity is also essential in the training of new leaders. Fostering an environment where calculated risk-taking, critical thinking, and generating new ideas are valued encourages innovative leadership. Emerging leaders must feel empowered to challenge the status quo and propose novel solutions, contributing to a dynamic and adaptive organizational culture.

Additionally, creating leaders involves building a strong support network. Facilitating collaboration among emerging leaders and providing opportunities to build connections with established leaders and among peers strengthens the leadership community. These connections not only offer informal mentoring, but also contribute to the exchange of knowledge and the building of valuable relationships in the career path of new leaders.

In short, creating new leaders goes beyond developing technical skills, including emotional intelligence, exposure to different experiences, promoting innovation and building a strong support network. This holistic approach prepares emerging leaders for the challenges and responsibilities of leading in a dynamic and changing business environment.

/ Alejandro Rivera /